AENGUS AND THE GREAT MAGICAL TRACTOR ADVENTURE

Aengus and the Magical Tractor

Marcus X Dahl

Vistic Press

Dedicated to Aengus, who loves tractors and the countryside.

CONTENTS

Aengus and The Great Magical Tractor Adventure

Once upon a time, there lived a little boy named Aengus who lived in the busy city with his parents. As well as city things like cars and trucks and cranes, Aengus loved animals and adventures in nature. He really wanted to go out in the countryside.

One day, Aengus's parents decided they also needed a break from the hustle, bustle and dirt of the city, so they all packed their bags and set off for the countryside in their family car.

Aengus's clever Mama had booked for them to visit a farm and Aengus was very excited.

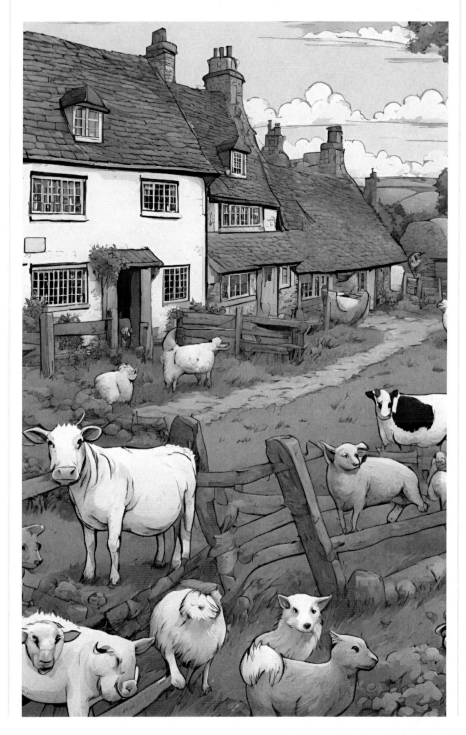

As they arrived at the beautiful old farm, Aengus's eyes widened with wonder. There were luxuriant fields of green, tall trees, and chirping birds everywhere.

But what caught Aengus's attention the most was a big red tractor standing by the barn. The tractor had huge back wheels, and small front wheels, all with wide knobbly tyres. The cabin was perched like a ship's bridge high up over the back wheels, and below that it had a large shiny steel tow-hitch for towing farm equipment.

"Wow!" exclaimed Aengus. "What a cool tractor!"

Little did Aengus know, but this was no ordinary tractor. This tractor's name was Terence, and he was a magical talking tractor!

"Hello there, young lad!" rumbled Terence in a friendly voice. "Welcome to the countryside! I'm Terence, the magical talking tractor. Would you like a tour around the farm?"

Aengus's eyes lit up with excitement. "Yes, please!" he exclaimed. His parents looked concerned, but when the friendly farmer Tim signalled to them that everything was ok, Aengus happily climbed aboard Terence, and they set off on their great tractor adventure. Terence's engine rumbled in a most satisfying way and sitting high up on the tractor, Aengus thought it was a bit like being sat on a big red elephant.

Terence guided Aengus around the farmyard, showing him all the amazing and beautiful things about the countryside. Aengus loved the swaying fields of wheat, the sound of the wind through the old English oak trees and the chirping of birds in the hedgerows.

As the tractor bumped and burbled slowly across the fields, Terence introduced Aengus to his other mechanical friends – the Harrow for tilling the soil and preparing for planting crops, the Baler for compressing the huge hay bales, the Mower for cutting grass, the Cultivator for breaking up soil, and the Sprayer for applying fertilizer. Terence explained that each machine had an important job to do, helping to grow the food that everyone eats.

"There's no food without us farmers" roared Terence merrily, with a puff of smoke from his mighty engine.

As they toured the farm, Terence also taught Aengus what to look out for, like horse troughs and animal feeders (don't fall in them!) and all the different animals – cows, sheep, pigs, horses, chickens, ducks, and geese (not to mention the dogs and cats). Aengus loved it when Terence honked his horn and the grumpy geese honked back, raising their beaks in the air. HONK HONK HONK!

They also met Daisy the cow, who lazily chewed her cud while basking in the warm sunshine. Nearby, fluffy white sheep grazed peacefully in the meadow. 'They'll need shearing soon!' said Terence.

"Otherwise they'll be too hot in the summer" said Aengus.

"Exactly!" Terence burbled happily. "And we can use their wool to make snuggly jumpers and coats to keep us warm in the winter".

"Oh yes!" said Aengus, thinking of how nice it is to be cosy in winter.

Terence also took Aengus to see the chicken coop, where they met a friendly hen named Henrietta, who proudly showed off her clutch of newly laid eggs. "Eggs are yummy and very good for you" said Terence, "though I myself only really drink diesel. MMM. Delicious!"

"And I only eat the yellow bits of eggs!" said Aengus guiltily, thinking about how his Mama tried so hard to get him to eat ALL of the delicious egg.

"And over there," said Terence continuing his tour, "see those holes beneath the hedgerow? That's the home of our mischievous digging friends, the badgers. We must be careful not to disturb them! They'll be sleeping now, but in the night-time they'll come out and forage for food".

"Badgers are one of my favourite animals" said Aengus excitedly. Terence laughed and a ring of smoke puffed out of his exhaust.

Lastly, they came to a big tin shed in the corner of the farm. "And this," said Terence proudly, "is where I sleep at night, cozy beside my best friend, the giant combine harvester, King Charles".

"Wow!" said Aengus, "he's HUGE!"

"He certainly is", said Terence, "and he's one of the most important machines on the farm – he helps harvest all our grain crops like wheat, corn and barley - but be quiet now as he's resting – it's his day off!"

Aengus was amazed by everything he had seen and learned. He felt so lucky to have made friends with such a special tractor.

After their long day, Aengus was feeling tired, and so he and his parents prepared to head back to the city. Aengus already couldn't wait to go back to the countryside again to see all his new friends.

"Thanks so much for the tour Terence!" he yelled out as he climbed into the car.

"Come again soon!" boomed Terence. "Think of us when you eat your food!"

"I will!" shouted Aengus.

As their car drove off, feeling sad and happy at the same time, Aengus waved goodbye to Terence and the farm, knowing that he would be back again someday soon to have another Great Tractor Adventure.

Manufactured by Amazon.ca
Acheson, AB

13226429R00015